Holidays

Earth Day

by Erika S. Manley

Bullfrog Books

Ideas for Parents and Teachers

Bullfrog Books let children practice reading informational text at the earliest reading levels. Repetition, familiar words, and photo labels support early readers.

Before Reading

- Discuss the cover photo. What does it tell them?
- Look at the picture glossary together. Read and discuss the words.

Read the Book

- "Walk" through the book and look at the photos. Let the child ask questions. Point out the photo labels.
- Read the book to the child, or have him or her read independently.

After Reading

- Prompt the child to think more. Ask: Do you celebrate Earth Day? What do you do?

Bullfrog Books are published by Jump!
5357 Penn Avenue South
Minneapolis, MN 55419
www.jumplibrary.com

Library of Congress Cataloging-in-Publication Data

Names: Manley, Erika S., author.
Title: Earth day / by Erika S. Manley.
Description: Minneapolis, Minnesota : Jump!, Inc., 2018. | Series: Holidays | Includes index.
Identifiers: LCCN 2017032850 (print)
LCCN 2017019275 (ebook) | ISBN 9781624966644 (ebook) | ISBN 9781620318300 (hardcover : alk. paper) | ISBN 9781620318317 (pbk.)
Subjects: LCSH: Earth Day—Juvenile literature.
Classification: LCC GE195.5 (print)
LCC GE195.5 .M35 2017 (ebook) | DDC 394.262—dc23
LC record available at https://lccn.loc.gov/2017032850

Editors: Jenny Fretland VanVoorst & Jenna Trnka
Book Designer: Leah Sanders
Photo Researcher: Leah Sanders

Photo Credits: Paul Hakimata Photography/Shutterstock, cover; wavebreakmedia/Shutterstock, 1, 24; Stieber/Shutterstock, 3; Hero Images/Getty, 4; asiseeit/iStock, 5; Sergei Bachlakov/Shutterstock, 6–7, 23tl; Rusla Ruseyn/Shutterstock, 8–9; Top Photo Group/Alamy, 10–11; A3pfamily/Shutterstock, 12–13; if/iStock, 14; kali9/iStock, 15; holgs/iStock, 16–17; Jamie Grill/Getty, 18; romrodinka/iStock, 19; FatCamera/iStock, 20–21, 23bl; JAJMO/iStock, 22tl; PeopleImages/iStock, 22tr; Serg64/Shutterstock, 22bl; Filipe B. Varela/Shutterstock, 22br, 23br; Npeter/Shutterstock, 23tr.

Printed in the United States of America at Corporate Graphics in North Mankato, Minnesota.

Table of Contents

What Is Earth Day?

Earth Day
is April 22.

It is a day to
care for Earth.

Earth Day started in 1970.
People in many countries
celebrate it.

Why?

Caring for Earth
is important.

We need fresh air.

We need clean water.

We need healthy soil.

How do we celebrate?
Ty's class does a craft.

11

Mac and Meg
plant a tree.

tree

13

Nic and Ivy pick up trash.

14

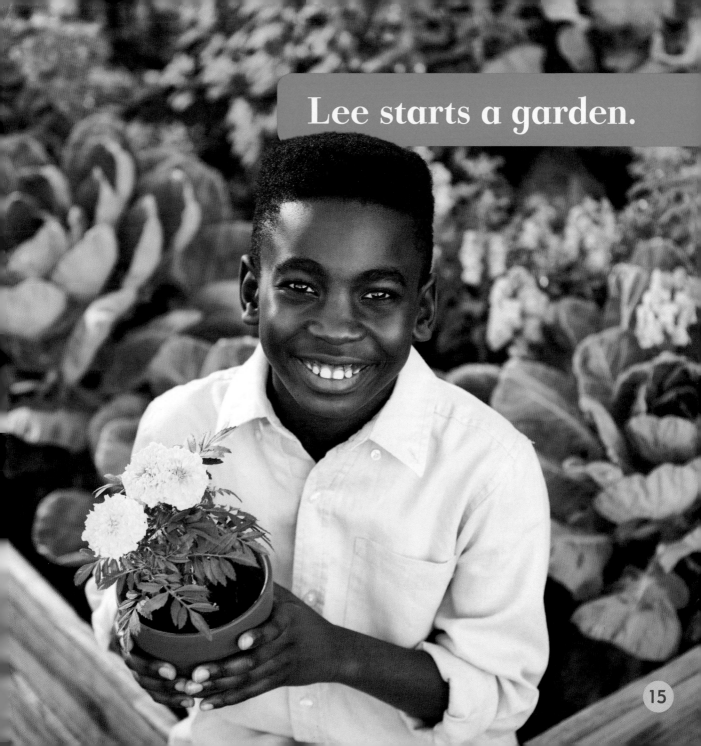

Lee starts a garden.

15

We can help Earth
every day.

How?

By making good
choices.

Bea reuses a
water bottle.

Rae turns off
the lights.

Tim bikes to school.

Earth is our home.

It feels good
to care for it.

Thank you, Earth!

You Can Help Earth!

Reusing water bottles cuts down on waste.

Conserve water by turning off the tap if you're not using the water.

Planting trees helps our air. Trees make oxygen and clean the air.

Keeping the ground clean keeps soil healthy. Healthy soil allows us to grow food.

Picture Glossary

celebrate
To observe in
a special way.

Earth
The planet
we live on.

craft
An activity
involving skill
in making things
by hand.

soil
Another word
for dirt.

Index

To Learn More

Learning more is as easy as 1, 2, 3.

1) Go to www.factsurfer.com

2) Enter "EarthDay" into the search box.

3) Click the "Surf" button to see a list of websites.

With factsurfer.com, finding more information is just a click away.